Hello, Summer!

Kari-Lynn Winters

Literacy Consultants
David Booth • Kathleen Corrigan

It is summer.

It can be very hot outside.

People and animals
need to stay cool.

It is summer.

Moose need to stay cool.

They swim in the lake.

It is summer.

Birds need to stay cool.

They splash in the birdbath.

It is summer.
Some plants need
to stay cool.

8

The roots need water.

The leaves need water.

The water helps the plants grow.

It is summer.

People need to stay cool.

We drink lots of water.

We play

in the water park.

We go on the slide.

We swim in the pool.

What do you do in the summer?